ARTIFICIAL INTELLIC

COLLECTION

DATA GOVERNANCE WITH AI

VOLUME 3

DEPLOYMENT GUIDE

Prof. Marcão - Marcus Vinícius Pinto

Disclaimer:

ISBN: 9798344394701

Publishing imprint: Independently published

Foreword

The era of Artificial Intelligence (AI) is not only built with sophisticated algorithms, but, above all, with the quality, integrity, and security of the data that feeds these systems.

At the heart of this revolution is data governance — a practice that transcends common management and imposes discipline, structure, and strategic alignment on the information that moves organizations.

This third volume of the "Data Governance with AI" collection, titled "Data Governance with AI — Volume 3: Deployment Guide," is an indispensable resource for any professional who needs to understand how to implement data governance in AI environments.

More than just technical reading, this book is designed to offer a practical, detailed, and structured guide, leading the reader to a deep understanding of each step involved in implementing effective data governance.

Who is this book for?

If you're a data scientist, data engineer, IT manager, systems auditor, or compliance and security professional, this book is written with you in mind.

The complexity of the AI ecosystem requires a solid approach to data management, and that's exactly what this book offers.

For data scientists and engineers, it provides the technical and strategic foundation needed for data architecture to be successfully deployed, ensuring that AI models can operate with reliable and consistent data.

For IT managers and auditors, the book provides a clear overview of best practices for ensuring data is aligned with compliance and security regulations, minimizing risk and increasing operational efficiency.

Organized into topics, the book covers everything from the principles of governance versus data management to the implementation of critical areas such as database operations management, data security, data quality, and metadata.

Each chapter provides insights into the actors responsible for these managements and the key aspects for the success of the implementation. Practical focus permeates each section, with clear and detailed guidance, leading the reader down a safe path from conception to full implementation of data governance.

This volume is not just a technical guide, but a strategic tool for leaders and professionals who are on the front lines of digital transformation. The practices discussed here are not theoretical; are applicable and adaptable to business realities.

And the impact of well-implemented data governance isn't limited to the IT environment. It is directly reflected in business results, the capacity for innovation, and the trust that the organization can build with its stakeholders.

However, this is just one step in an essential journey in the field of artificial intelligence. This volume is part of a larger collection, "Artificial Intelligence: The Power of Data," which explores, in depth, different aspects of AI and data science.

The other volumes address equally crucial topics, such as the integration of AI systems, predictive analytics, and the use of advanced algorithms for decision-making.

By purchasing and exploring the rest of the books in the collection, you'll get a complete and detailed look at the critical elements shaping the future of AI and data management. This collection gives you the intellectual tools you need to transform your organization and put it at the forefront of the digital revolution.

Get ready for a rich and transformative read. The future of AI starts with data — and you're about to master it.

Happy reading!
Good learning!

Prof. Marcão - Marcus Vinícius Pinto

Digital influencer specializing in soft skills for professional fulfillment of entrepreneurs, entrepreneurs, leaders and managers. Founder, CEO, teacher and pedagogical advisor at MVP Consult.

Summary

1. Introduction.

In the vast world of data governance, it is imperative to have a comprehensive and structured perspective to navigate the complexities and challenges inherent in this area.

In this text, we enter an unknown universe, diving headlong into fundamental concepts and practices that will reinvigorate the way we understand and manage data.

With an emphasis on the DAMA International Data Governance Framework, this work presents a sophisticated view of governance, data model auditing, abbreviations, and the histories of companies and institutions that have been consolidated through efficient information management over the centuries.

Striving for excellence in data governance transcends the immediate value that data can provide. We are confronted with the understanding that data is like crude oil, with no value on its own.

It is only through effective governance, careful analysis, and proper application of information architecture concepts that we can distill this crude oil into liquid gold, generating substantial value and positive impact on our organizations.

Inspired by the impactful words of Microsoft CEO Satya Nadella, we are driven to deeply question the role of data in our lives and the importance of governing it wisely.

Entering the chapters of this book, you will have access to a world of structured knowledge, where data governance stands as the foundation of efficient and sustainable management.

Through practical examples and theoretical background, you will understand how the fundamentals of governance are applied in practice and how we can effectively design structures to meet the needs of our organizations.

Auditing data models, an extremely relevant aspect of information management, plays a crucial role in our relentless search for reliability and quality.

In this book, we will explore the potential of this indispensable practice, discovering better ways to identify and correct failures, ensuring the integrity of information systems, and mitigating risks.

With a practical and detailed approach, we will learn how to apply the most advanced auditing techniques, which will play an essential role in our efforts to ensure the accuracy and security of our valuable data.

As we unravel the mysteries of organizations' abbreviations and histories, we are immersed in a journey through time, walking among the visionary steps of great leaders who shared a vision of the importance of data and left a lasting legacy.

Their stories will inspire us to raise our own standards, enhancing data governance and accelerating our pursuit of excellence.

As policies and standards present in this guide was developed based on the guidelines of the DAMA International Data Governance Framework1 and the DAMA Data Management Dictionary2, we have:

---

1 Data Management Body of Knowledge.

2 DAMA Dictionary of Data Management.

1. Definition of responsibilities.
2. Policies and Procedures.
3. Data quality.
4. Information security.
5. Regulatory compliance.
6. Definition of responsibilities.
7. Policies and Procedures.
8. Data quality.
9. Information security.
10. Regulatory compliance.
11. Metadata management.

Each body or entity in an organization's structure is a fundamental part of this data governance system and must be responsible for implementing the actions described in this guide, ensuring its success.

DAMA International's Data Governance Framework refers to a set of practices and guidelines established by DAMA International, a non-profit organization dedicated to data management and governance.

This framework aims to provide guidance for effective data governance within organizations.

DAMA International is widely recognized as one of the leading authorities on data governance in the world. Its framework is based on fundamental principles, best practices, and industry standards.

It addresses various dimensions of data governance, including strategy, organization, architecture, integration, quality, security, and compliance.

DAMA International's Data Governance Framework began to gain prominence as a world reference in the area of data governance from its creation, which took place in 1980 in the United States.

The widespread adoption and global recognition of DAMA International's framework is a result of its effectiveness and ability to provide practical guidance for implementing data governance.

By following DAMA International's Data Governance Framework, organizations can establish a systematic process to manage their data assets efficiently, ensuring quality, security, and compliance across the enterprise.

This involves defining clear roles and responsibilities, creating policies and guidelines, establishing quality control processes, among other essential practices.

It is possible to observe the Practices contained in the DAMA Model, as well as the practices adapted to the context of the Municipality of Belo Horizonte that gave rise to the institution's Data Governance Model.

1   Data governance versus data management.

When it comes to data governance, it is important to differentiate it from data management due to the importance of these concepts in the area of information management. While some people may use these terms interchangeably, they have distinct definitions and goals.

In simple terms, data governance is the set of policies, processes, guidelines, and organizational structures that are established to ensure the effective and efficient use of data in an institution.

It aims to establish a framework of responsibilities and decision-making to ensure that data is properly managed, protected, properly used, and aligned with strategic objectives and applicable regulations.

Data governance is related to the definition of organizational policies regarding data quality, security, privacy, integrity, consistency, and usability.

It involves creating rules and regulations to guide data collection, storage, maintenance, sharing, and disposal activities throughout its lifecycle.

In addition, data governance also deals with defining roles and responsibilities for relevant stakeholders, as well as monitoring and compliance mechanisms.

Data management focuses on the operational aspects of information management. It encompasses the practical activities involved in collecting, storing, organizing, cleaning, analyzing, and using data to support business processes and make informed decisions.

Data management involves the use of technologies, tools, and methodologies to ensure that data is correctly structured, standardized, and available to authorized users.

Data management encompasses maintaining databases, implementing security and backup policies, integrating data from different sources, ensuring data quality, and making relevant information available to stakeholders.

It focuses on the day-to-day operational management of data, aiming to ensure that it is up-to-date, correct, accessible, and delivered in the right format at the right time.

It can be concluded that data governance defines the guidelines and organizational structures to ensure effective data management, while data management focuses on practical and operational activities related to the collection, storage, organization, and daily use of data.

These two concepts are interrelated and complementary, as effective governance is essential to ensure the success of data management in any institution.

2   Implementation of data governance.

"Data governance is the process by which
organizations exercise authority and
control over data management."
Sid Adelman.[3]

There is a question that directs the entire process of implementing data governance in an institution.

This question is

---

*WHAT DOES THE COMPANY WANT TO DO WITH
THE DATA?*

The answer to this question defines the data strategy and should be clear and easy to understand. If only one data scientist can understand the strategy, it is unlikely to be successful, if everyone wants to get on board. Data governance plays a key role in supporting this strategy at every stage.

But before data governance can support this strategy, data governance must be implemented.

---

[3] Sid Adelman is a renowned expert in data governance and data quality, being one of the pioneers and influencers in this area. The quote highlights the importance of data governance to ensure the quality, integrity, security, and compliance of data within an organization, promoting strategic and effective decision-making based on reliable information.

Let's take a look at the ten thematic areas for implementing data governance:

2.1   Implementing data architecture management.

At the institution, data architecture management plays a key role in data governance. The implementation of this process aims to ensure the quality, integrity, and availability of information throughout the institution.

To begin with, it is essential that there is a clear understanding of the institution's goals and needs regarding data. This involves identifying what data is relevant to the public administration, how it is collected, stored, and shared, as well as defining the standards and guidelines for its use.

Data architecture is then established as a set of guidelines, policies, techniques, and tools that guide the institution and management of the data.

This includes defining standardized data models, storage structures, data capture and transformation processes, as well as establishing security and privacy protocols.

The implementation of data architecture management is an ongoing effort, which requires the collaboration and engagement of different areas of the institution. It is necessary to involve data managers, IT teams, information security professionals, and those responsible for privacy policies.

A key aspect is the cataloging of data, that is, documenting and categorizing all the datasets available in the institution.

This enables a better understanding of existing data, facilitates information sharing across departments, and helps avoid unnecessary duplication of effort in data collection and analysis.

In addition, managing data architecture involves defining clear responsibilities. It is essential to assign roles and responsibilities to the professionals involved, such as data managers, data architects, database administrators, and data analysts.

They will be responsible for ensuring that the established standards and guidelines are followed and implemented correctly.

Another important point is the guarantee of data quality. This involves conducting periodic audits, resolving data integrity and consistency issues, and monitoring the performance of data management systems.

Finally, data governance must be an adaptive and evolutionary process. It is critical that the data architecture is reviewed and updated regularly, taking into account changing needs

In this way, the implementation of data architecture management in the institution's data governance will ensure a solid basis for decision-making, promoting a more efficient, transparent, and reliable data-driven public administration.

2.1.1   Key aspects.

Deploying data architecture management in data governance requires consideration of several essential prerequisites that must be addressed before implementing data architecture management, such as:

1. Understanding of goals and needs. Before implementing data architecture management, it is essential to have a clear understanding of the objectives and needs of public administration. This involves identifying what data is relevant to the institution, how it is collected, stored, and shared, as well as defining the standards and guidelines for its use.

2. Definition of a data governance strategy. The institution must establish a clear data governance strategy, in which the management of the data architecture is inserted. This strategy should outline the objectives, goals, and principles that will guide data governance, as well as identify the roles and responsibilities of the various actors involved.

3. Establishment of a dedicated data management team. The institution must assemble a team specialized in data management, made up of professionals trained in data architecture, governance, and data quality. This team will be responsible for implementing and maintaining the data architecture, ensuring its compliance with data governance guidelines.

4. Cataloguing of data. It is necessary to carry out a complete cataloguing of the data available at the institution. This involves documenting and categorizing all datasets, identifying their meaning, origin, format, and relationships. Data cataloging facilitates the management and sharing of information, avoiding unnecessary duplication of efforts.

5. Definition of standards and guidelines. The institution must establish clear standards and guidelines for data architecture. This includes defining standardized data models, storage structures, data capture and transformation processes, as well as establishing security and privacy protocols.

6. Investment in infrastructure and technology. It is essential that the institution invests in adequate infrastructure and technology to support the management of the data architecture. This includes the adoption of efficient data management systems, data analysis and visualization tools, as well as security and data protection mechanisms.

7. Skills development. The institution must invest in the development of data management skills among its professionals. This involves training and qualification for managers, analysts, and IT staff, ensuring that they have the necessary knowledge to implement and maintain the data architecture effectively.

2.2 Implementing data development.

To implement data development in the institution's data governance, the following steps are required:

1. Identification of data needs. It is critical to understand the needs of different departments and end-users in the institution regarding data. This requires a detailed analysis to identify what information is relevant, how it will be used, and what quality and integrity requirements must be met.

2. Planning and structuring of data. Based on the identified needs, it is necessary to plan and structure the data in a consistent and standardized way. This involves defining data models, storage formats, naming standards, and integration strategies.

3. Data collection and processing. At this stage, data is collected, either through internal or external sources to the institution. Once collected, the data goes through cleaning, validation, transformation and enrichment processes, ensuring its quality and consistency.

4. Data storage and management. Proper data storage and management infrastructure is essential. The institution must implement efficient and scalable database management systems that ensure data availability, integrity, and security.

5. Availability and sharing of data. The institution's data governance should promote the availability and efficient sharing of data. This

can be done through portals, APIs, or other forms of secure access to data, following established security and privacy protocols.

6. Monitoring and ensuring data quality. It is crucial to continuously monitor the quality of the data to ensure its integrity and reliability. The institution must establish quality indicators, conduct periodic audits, and implement mechanisms for early detection of anomalies or inconsistencies in the data.

7. Evolution and continuous improvement of data. Data development should be an ongoing process, adapting to changing needs and demands Data governance should promote innovation and continuous improvement, seeking to update and improve data infrastructure, processes, and strategies.

In order to be able to have the dimension of diversity and richness of the data of an entity the size of the City of Belo Horizonte, this document presents the list of tables of the conceptual corporate model implemented in the Open Data Portal.

ANNEX II presents the structure of the tables of the institution's Corporate Open Data Portal Model. This model was created to organize and make more accessible the information available on the Open Data Portal of the City of Belo Horizonte (institution).

The structure of the tables was prepared taking into account the needs of data governance and the standardization of information. Each table represents a specific data set, and its attributes were selected according to criteria of relevance and usefulness to users.

The Corporate Model of Open Data Portal is composed of several tables that cover different areas, such as education, health, transportation, environment, among others. Each table has a consistent structure, with columns that represent the attributes of the information made available.

The attributes present in each table are organized in a hierarchical way, allowing for a better understanding and ease of use of the data. In addition, the structure of the tables follows good data modeling practices, such as normalization, thus ensuring the consistency and integrity of the information.

2.2.1 Actors in the development of data.

The institution's data governance involves a number of actors working together to ensure that data is managed effectively and is available to support decision-making and day-to-day activities.

1. Data managers. These professionals are in charge of organizing and managing the institution's data. They oversee the collection, storage, integrity, security, and access to this data. Data managers have a responsibility to ensure that data is available and can be used reliably throughout the institution.

2. Servers in the business areas. These actors are the experts in their respective fields and have a deep understanding of the data needs for decision-making. They work together with data managers to define requirements and ensure that data is relevant and useful to their daily activities.

3. Application and system developers. They are responsible for creating and maintaining the systems and applications that utilize the governed data. Developers play a key role in implementing data governance policies and ensuring the quality of the data used by these applications.

4. Users of the data. These can be the citizens and companies that consume information made available by the institution. Engaging and raising awareness of these actors about the importance of data governance is essential to ensure adherence to the process.

5. Managers. They have the responsibility to provide the necessary support for the implementation of data governance by providing sufficient resources and establishing an organizational culture that values quality data and data-driven decision-making.

2.2.2   Key aspects.

For the successful deployment of data development in the institution's data governance, some prerequisites must be considered:

1. Commitment of senior management. It is essential that the institution's leadership is committed and engaged in the data governance process. This involves understanding the importance of data and actively supporting the implementation of an effective strategy.

2. Definition of policies and guidelines. It is necessary to establish clear policies and guidelines for data development in the institution's data governance. These guidelines should address aspects such as data quality, information security, data privacy, among others.

3. Appropriate organizational structure. The institution needs to create an appropriate organizational structure to promote data governance. This may include assigning a team responsible for data governance, with well-defined roles and responsibilities.

4. Evaluation and management of existing data. Before starting data development in institution data governance, it is important to conduct an evaluation of existing data. This involves identifying quality issues, standardizing, and cleaning data if necessary.

5. Appropriate tools and technologies. The institution must invest in appropriate tools and technologies for data development. This can include implementing an efficient data management system, using advanced data analysis techniques, and adopting robust security practices.

6. Training and awareness. Employee empowerment plays a key role in implementing data development into the institution's data

governance. Employees should receive appropriate training on data governance policies, guidelines, and best practices.

7. Continuous monitoring and review. Data governance is an ongoing process. The institution should establish regular monitoring and review mechanisms to ensure that data development policies and practices are updated in line with evolving needs.

2.3 Implementing the operations management of the database management system,

The implementation of DBMS Operations Management in the institution's data governance will be carried out in several stages. First, a detailed survey of the institution's requirements and needs will be made in relation to the data stored in its systems. This includes identifying critical data, its origin, format, and security requirements.

Based on this information, policies and guidelines will be established for the safe and efficient management of databases. This will involve setting security standards, such as authentication and encryption, to protect data from unauthorized access.

In addition, data backup and recovery routines will be established to ensure data availability and integrity. A backup strategy will be defined that meets business requirements and allows data recovery in the event of a failure or disaster.

Another important aspect of DBMS Operations Management will be the continuous monitoring of databases. Monitoring systems will be implemented to track performance, identify potential issues, and ensure optimal use of hardware resources.

In addition, the team responsible for DBMS Operations Management must be prepared to deal with security incidents, such as cyber attacks or data breaches. Incident response mechanisms will be established to ensure swift and efficient action in emergency situations.

2.3.1 Actors in the management of operations of the database management system.

The actors in the management of database manager operations in the institution's data governance are specialized professionals who work in the administration, maintenance and evolution of the databases used by the institution.

These professionals have the responsibility to ensure the integrity, security, availability, and performance of data, as well as to promote proper access and compliance with established governance policies.

Among the actors involved in this process, the following stand out:

1. Database Administrator. The database administrator is the professional responsible for managing the database environment, including the installation, configuration, maintenance, and monitoring of the servers and related systems. It takes care of the organization and structuring of data, as well as the definition of access and security rules.

2. Data Analyst. The data analyst is responsible for understanding the institution's needs regarding the data and translating them into rules and models that are implemented in the database. It works closely with end-users to define requirements and ensure that data is properly structured and available to support the institution's operations.

3. IT Project Manager. The IT project manager plays an important role in data governance, ensuring that projects related to the database manager are aligned with established strategies and policies. He coordinates the development and deployment teams, ensuring that deadlines are met and quality requirements are met.

4. Development Team. The development team is responsible for implementing the software solutions that utilize the database. These professionals work together with the data analyst to create the desired structures, queries, and functionalities, always respecting governance guidelines and policies.

5. End Users. End users are those who interact with the database manager on a daily basis and depend on the data stored in it to perform their activities. They have the responsibility to use the data correctly and in accordance with the institution's governance policies.

2.3.2   Key aspects.

The implementation of DBMS operations management in the institution's data governance requires some prerequisites that are essential to ensure the success and effectiveness of this process.

These prerequisites are related to technical, organizational, and human resources aspects.

Let's explore some of them:

1. IT infrastructure. It is essential to have an adequate IT infrastructure to support the implementation of DBMS operations management. This involves the availability of servers, networks, storage, and other resources necessary to ensure data performance, security, and availability.

2. DBMS specialists. The institution must have professionals specialized in DBMS, such as database administrators, data analysts, and developers, who have the necessary knowledge to effectively manage and operate the system. These experts must be able to handle the specific demands of the institution's data governance.

3. Definition of policies and guidelines. Setting clear policies and guidelines related to data governance is essential. This includes establishing guidelines for the structuring, security, access, and use of data stored in the DBMS. These policies must be communicated and disseminated to all those involved in the process, ensuring a common understanding and alignment of actions.

4. Alignment with organizational strategies. The implementation of the DBMS operations management must be aligned with the institution's organizational strategies and objectives. It is important that data governance is considered as an integral part of the institution's strategic plan, aiming to improve the quality, availability, and proper use of data.

5. Capacity building and training. The qualification and training of professionals involved in data governance are essential to ensure the knowledge and competence necessary to deal with the operations of the DBMS. The institution must invest in training programs and continuous training, aiming to update and improve the skills of its staff.

6. Data culture. The existence of an organizational culture that values and prioritizes data governance is essential. All employees of the institution must understand the importance of data, as well as the benefits and responsibilities of its proper management. This involves raising awareness about the quality of the data, compliance with established policies, and the strategic value that the data holds for the institution.

2.4   Implementing data security management.

Data security management plays a key role in data governance. With the support of the institution, the implementation of the appropriate security mechanisms will ensure the protection of data against internal and external threats, as well as compliance with established guidelines and regulations.

Implementing data security management into the institution's data governance will involve several steps and approaches, including:

1. Risk assessment and analysis. A thorough risk assessment will be carried out in relation to the data stored and processed by the institution. This will involve identifying potential threats, vulnerabilities, and impacts on data. Based on this analysis, appropriate security measures will be defined.

2. Security policies and guidelines. Clear policies and guidelines related to data security will be established. This will include setting standards for authentication, encryption, access control, monitoring, and auditing, among others. These policies and guidelines must be communicated and disseminated to all those involved, ensuring compliance and alignment of actions.

3. Security controls. Security controls will be implemented, such as firewalls, intrusion detection and prevention systems, antivirus, multi-factor authentication, among others. These controls aim to protect data from unauthorized access, malware, and other potential threats.

4. Training and awareness. Training and awareness of the institution's employees in relation to data security practices will be carried out. This will include education on the importance of data security, best practices for use and protection, and individual responsibilities to ensure data security.

5. Monitoring and auditing. Continuous monitoring and auditing mechanisms will be implemented to track compliance with established security policies and guidelines. This will include analyzing access logs, anomaly detection, periodic reviews, and vulnerability testing.

6. Incident management. A structured process for dealing with data security incidents will be established. This will involve defining responsibilities, taking swift and appropriate action to mitigate any identified threats, and continuous learning to prevent similar incidents in the future.

2.4.1 Data security management actors.

Data security management is a key concern in an institution's operations, especially when it comes to the public sector. The institution must recognize the importance of ensuring the confidentiality, integrity, and availability of the data circulating in its system, as well as the need to comply with current regulations, such as the General Data Protection Law.

This process involves different actors, each playing a specific role in the protection and responsible management of information:

1. Executive Leadership. Executive leadership, represented by the institution's managers and decision-makers, plays a key role in promoting a culture of data security. They establish the strategic vision, allocate resources, and set the policies. Additionally, it is the responsibility of executive leadership to ensure that safety guidelines are communicated and implemented throughout the institution.

2. Information Technology (IT) Team. The IT team is responsible for implementing and maintaining information security systems. They perform risk analysis, establish controls, and ensure that the technological solutions used by the institution meet security

requirements. This team is also responsible for identifying and responding to security incidents, as well as keeping systems up-to-date with the latest threat protections.

3. Data Professionals. Data professionals play a key role in data governance. They define security policies, classify and categorize data, establish access controls, and ensure compliance with regulations. In addition, they work closely with IT staff to ensure that data is protected throughout its lifecycle, from collection to storage and deletion.

4. End Users. All employees of the institution who deal with personal data or sensitive information are important actors in the management of data security. They should receive appropriate training on security policies and best practices, as well as be made aware of the importance of protecting the data they handle on a daily basis. By acting diligently, end users can help prevent security incidents and ensure citizen privacy.

5. Internal Control Body. The internal control body is responsible for monitoring and evaluating the effectiveness of the security measures implemented in data governance. They audit processes, identify gaps, and recommend improvements. This body acts as an independent verification mechanism, ensuring that security policies and controls are being followed in accordance with best practices.

2.4.2   Key aspects.

Implementing effective data governance is critical to ensuring information security in an institution, especially when it comes to sensitive and confidential municipal government data.

The institution must commit to establishing the necessary prerequisites for data security management.

First and foremost, data security awareness should be spread throughout the institution. This involves regular training, workshops, and internal communications to make employees aware of security best practices, the risks associated with improper data handling, and how to identify potential threats.

Next, it is necessary to establish clear and well-defined data security policies. These policies should address aspects such as the classification of data according to its level of sensitivity, restrictions on access to data, the use of encryption and other protective measures, as well as guidelines for identifying and responding to security incidents.

In addition to policies, it is important to invest in appropriate technologies and infrastructure to support data security. This includes the use of firewalls, intrusion detection and prevention systems, two-factor authentication, regularly updated backups, among other features that help protect data from external and internal threats.

Another crucial prerequisite is the establishment of a business continuity and disaster recovery plan. This ensures that in the event of serious incidents such as cyberattacks, there are clear processes and procedures in place to recover the lost or compromised data, minimizing the impact on government operations and public trust.

Finally, it is necessary to conduct regular audits to validate the effectiveness of the security measures implemented.

Audits should review existing security controls, identify potential gaps or vulnerabilities, and propose necessary improvements and updates to strengthen data security management.

2.5 Implementing master data management (mdm) and reference data management (rdm).

The implementation of master and reference data management in the institution's data governance will follow a few key steps.

First, a thorough analysis of existing data will be conducted, identifying data sources, source systems, and potential gaps or inconsistencies. This will help gain a comprehensive understanding of the data involved and its respective needs.

Then, the mapping of the master and reference data necessary for the different areas of the municipal administration will be made.

This process involves identifying the most important data entities, such as citizens, businesses, locations, and other objects relevant to the institution's operations. In addition, the attributes associated with each entity will be defined and the necessary quality standards for this data will be established.

After mapping, a master and reference data management structure will be developed. This includes defining responsibilities and roles within the institution, as well as creating clear policies and guidelines for collecting, maintaining, and updating this data.

Governance processes will also be established to constantly monitor data quality, ensuring consistency and integrity over time.

For effective implementation, it is crucial to ensure collaboration between the different sectors of the institution.

The management of master and reference data requires a multidisciplinary approach, involving areas such as information technology, human resources, urban planning, health, education, among others.

Knowledge exchange and communication between these sectors will be encouraged to ensure that data governance is truly efficient and widely adopted.

Additionally, the implementation of master and reference data management will be supported by appropriate technologies such as data management systems and data quality tools.

These technologies will help automate processes, improve data consistency, and optimize the efficiency of the institution's data governance.

2.5.1   Master and reference data management actors.

The actors involved in master and reference data management have a responsibility to ensure the quality, integrity, and consistency of the data used within the municipal government.

One of the key players in this initiative is the master and reference data manager. This professional will have the role of leading the team in charge of consolidating, validating, and maintaining master data, which is the most important and critical information for the institution.

In addition, the master data manager will be responsible for defining the guidelines and policies related to the management of this data.

Another important player is the information architect, who will play a key role in data governance. This professional will be responsible for performing the technical administration of the systems used to store and manage master and reference data.

The information architect will be responsible for maintaining the necessary technological infrastructure, ensuring that the systems are in full operation and meeting security and integrity requirements.

In addition to these specific actors, data governance will have the participation of other professionals, such as data analysts, who will be responsible for analyzing and interpreting the data, providing relevant information for decision-making.

Developers will also play an important role in ensuring that information systems are developed in an appropriate manner, following the standards and guidelines established for the management of master and reference data.

Finally, the end users of the data will also be key players in this process. They must comply with the policies and guidelines defined by the institution's data governance, ensuring the updating and correct use of information.

2.5.2   Key aspects.

The prerequisites structure a solid foundation needed to establish an effective data governance framework and ensure the quality and integrity of the data used by the organization:

1. Clear understanding of master and reference data:

    -   Master data: Critical and consistent information across the organization, such as customers, suppliers, employees, and products.

    -   Reference data: used to standardize and validate master data, ensuring consistency and quality across different systems and processes.

2. Appropriate organizational structure to manage master and reference data:

    -   Definition of clear roles and responsibilities for the teams involved in the process.

- Interconnected teams working collaboratively to validate, update, and maintain data consistency.

3. Data management policies and procedures:

   - Clear guidelines for collecting, storing, organizing, updating, and disposing of data.

   - Data governance rules, such as naming, formatting, and quality standards.

4. Adequate technological support:

   - Implementation of data quality systems and tools to validate, correct, and maintain data.

   - Robust and secure information technology infrastructure to ensure data availability and protection.

5. Employee education and training:

   - Empower employees with the skills and knowledge needed to maintain data quality and accuracy.

   - Specific training, workshops and sharing of good practices.

2.6 Implementing data warehouse management and business intelligence.

The Data Warehouse is a centralized environment that stores data from different sources in a structured, organized, and integrated way. It aims to serve as a basis for decision-making, providing consistent and reliable information.

In the institution's data governance, the DW will be implemented to consolidate data from various areas, such as health, education, public finance, among others, seeking to create a unified and comprehensive view of the data.

Business Intelligence, in turn, is the set of techniques and tools that allow the analysis and exploitation of data stored in DW. Through BI, it will be possible to extract relevant insights, identify trends, analyze performance indicators, and generate interactive reports and dashboards to assist in decision-making.

In the implementation of the institution's data governance, DW and BI will be integrated into the management system, collecting data from different sources, consolidating it and making it available for analysis.

The responsible team will carry out the data modeling, defining the key points that will be monitored and establishing the relevant indicators for the areas of public management.

It will also be necessary to define the metrics to be monitored and the reports to be generated. Through DW and BI, it will be possible to monitor the performance of public services, identify bottlenecks, analyze the effectiveness of public policies, among other aspects, in order to promote continuous improvement and efficiency in decision-making.

It is important to note that the successful implementation of DW and BI in the institution's data governance requires the involvement of a multidisciplinary team, which includes professionals from areas such as information technology, public management, and data analysis.

In addition, it is essential to have a defined governance structure, with clear roles and responsibilities, that ensure the security and ethical use of data.

In this way, by implementing DW and BI in the institution's data governance, it will be possible to obtain a holistic view of the data and transform it into valuable information to improve public services, promote transparency and efficiency in municipal management.

2.6.1   Data warehouse management and business intelligence actors.

There are several key players involved in these areas.

Here are the main ones:

1. Project managers: are responsible for leading and managing data warehouse and business intelligence implementation projects. They coordinate teams, set deadlines, necessary resources, and ensure that objectives are met.

2. Data warehouse architects: These are the experts in designing the structure and data flows of the data warehouse. They create the dimensional models and establish the strategies for extracting, transforming, and loading (etl) the data coming from different sources.

3. ETL developers: These are the professionals in charge of building the ETL processes. They extract the data from various sources, apply necessary transformations, and load the data into dw efficiently and securely.

4. Business intelligence analysts: they are responsible for creating and maintaining reports, dashboards, and dashboards in business intelligence. They work collaboratively with end-users to understand their needs, turning data into relevant information and presenting clear visualizations to decision-makers.

5. Data security specialists: These are the professionals who focus on protecting the data stored in dw. They implement security measures, such as encryption, access control, and auditing, to ensure the integrity and confidentiality of the data.

6. End users: These are the people who use the information made available by the data warehouse and business intelligence for operational and strategic purposes. They keep track of reports, perform ad hoc analysis, and utilize BI tools to gain actionable insights that can impact decision-making.

2.6.2   Key aspects.

The adoption of an appropriate methodology is essential for the successful management of Data Warehouse and Business Intelligence in the institution's data governance.

The implementation and operationalization of these technologies require the consideration of several prerequisites, and an effective methodology is the main one.

It is essential to have a methodological approach in DW and BI management that contemplates the following prerequisites:

1. Detailed planning.

Before starting the implementation of DW and BI, it is essential to have a detailed plan that lays out clear goals and objectives.

The methodology must include processes to structure the planning, identify the necessary steps, the resources allocated, and the deadlines to be met.

2. Robust infrastructure.

A solid technology infrastructure is critical to supporting DW and BI. The methodology should assist in defining the needs for hardware, software, networks, and storage capacity, ensuring that the infrastructure is appropriately sized to support the demands of data and queries.

3. Proper modeling and design.

The methodology should be able to define a structured approach to DW modeling and design. This includes defining dimensions, facts, and relationships between data in a consistent way, ensuring the integrity and accuracy of the information made available by the system.

4. Data quality.

The methodology must ensure the quality of the data stored in the DW. Through well-defined processes, the methodology will help standardize, clean, and validate data, ensuring that only reliable and consistent information is used in decision-making.

5. Security and privacy.

The methodology should assist in the definition of policies and controls to ensure data security and privacy. Access, authentication, and encryption standards will be established, taking into account applicable regulations and guidelines.

6. Integration of data sources.

The methodology should provide guidelines and procedures for integrating various data sources into DW. This involves defining extract, transform, and load (ETL) processes that are efficient and ensure consistency and freshness of data from different systems.

7. User training.

The methodology should also address the empowerment of users, providing the necessary training and resources so that they can effectively use DW and BI. This will help ensure that users are familiar with the system's functionalities, thus promoting greater adoption and utilization of the available information.

2.7   Implementing documentation and content management.

To implement documentation and content management in data governance in the institution, it is important to follow some essential steps.

Here are some guidelines:

1. Identify and classify the types of documentation and content. It is necessary to map and understand the various types of documents and content existing in the institution. This can include policies, guidelines, manuals, contracts, reports, among others. Classifying these documents according to their relevance and characteristics will allow for a more efficient organization.

2. Establish management guidelines and procedures. Defining clear guidelines and procedures for the management of documentation and content is essential. This includes establishing archiving policies, format standardization, version control, access levels, and document retention. These guidelines should be communicated and disseminated to everyone involved in data governance.

3. Implement a document management system. Using an appropriate document management system is essential to facilitate the organization, search, and retrieval of information. These systems can help with document centralization, version control, change tracking, and collaboration between users. Choosing a reliable solution that is adaptable to the needs of the institution will be essential.

4. Empower employees. It is important to invest in the training of employees involved in the management of documentation and content. This includes training on the established guidelines and procedures, as well as practical guidance on how to use the document management system. Awareness of the importance of

documentation needs to be disseminated throughout the organization.

5. Monitor and audit regularly. The implementation of documentation and content management must be accompanied by regular monitoring and audits to ensure adherence to established policies and procedures. This will help identify and correct any issues, as well as continuously improve the management system.

6. Promote the culture of document management. From the top management, it is necessary to promote a culture of appreciation and care with the management of documentation. This involves making employees aware of the importance of correct documentation, sharing information, and preserving records. Encouraging consistent documentation and content practices will be essential for robust data governance.

Documenting attributes is a key step in data governance, as it allows users to understand and correctly use the information made available. The Data Standard defined for this documentation establishes the information that must be provided for each attribute present in the Open Data Portal Enterprise Model tables.

This pattern includes information such as attribute name, description, data type, value constraints, format, and more. In addition, the Data Standard also establishes guidelines for documenting related attributes, such as foreign keys and relationships between tables.

By following the Data Standard for Attribute Documentation, the institution ensures consistency and clarity in the documentation of its Open Data Portal attributes. This facilitates the use of information by users and contributes to the transparency and effective governance of the data made available.

2.7.1   Actors in the management of documentation and content.

In the implementation of documentation and content management, the actors involved play a crucial role in the management of documentation and content.

They are:

1. Data Governance Team. This team is primarily responsible for developing and implementing data governance policies at the institution. It is composed of data experts and information technology professionals who have expertise in project management, information security, privacy, and compliance. These professionals are responsible for defining the standards and processes related to data documentation and content.

2. Information architects. Information architects are responsible for managing the structure of the database and ensuring data integrity and quality. They work closely with end users and the data governance team to understand the documentation and content requirements needed for each type of data. In addition, information architects establish policies for updating and maintaining metadata, promoting the proper management of the institution's data.

3. End Users. End users are the ultimate recipients of institution-governed data. They can include employees, managers, suppliers, citizens, and other stakeholders. To ensure effective management of documentation and content, it is critical that end users are aware of data governance policies and follow the guidelines established by the governance team. They are also responsible for providing feedback on the relevance and accuracy of the data, helping to continuously improve the quality of the documentation.

4. External Consultants. In some cases, the institution may engage external consultants who specialize in data governance to support

the implementation process. These professionals have advanced knowledge in the field and can help align the institution's practices with industry best practices.

2.7.2   Key aspects.

Managing documentation and content is an extensive and time-consuming job. Its main prerequisites are:

1. Develop a comprehensive inventory of all relevant documents and content in the organization, identifying the systems in which the data is stored and creating a classification structure to facilitate the organization and retrieval of information.

2. Define clear policies and procedures for creating, reviewing, approving, and publishing documents and content, including guidelines for the format, style, and structure of these materials, ensuring compliance with applicable laws and regulations.

3. Ensure the authenticity and integrity of documents and content through the implementation of access and version controls, as well as the definition of appropriate retention and disposal policies.

4. Perform constant monitoring and adopt a continuous improvement approach, regularly reviewing the documentation and content management processes, correcting identified problems and seeking ways to improve the system.

2.8   Implementing metadata management.

When implementing metadata management in the institution's data governance, some important steps must be considered:

1. Identification and definition of relevant metadata. The first step is to identify and define which metadata is relevant to the institution's data governance. This can include information about the data's source, context, quality, format, meaning, and other important attributes.

2. Cataloging and documentation of metadata. Once identified, metadata must be cataloged and documented in a structured manner. This may involve creating a metadata glossary, with clear and standardized definitions for each term used.

3. Implementation of metadata management tools. To facilitate the management and use of metadata, it is recommended to implement specific tools, such as metadata management systems or data catalogs. These tools assist in organizing, searching, and updating metadata as needed.

4. Mapping of relationships and dependencies. An important aspect of metadata management is the mapping of relationships and dependencies between the different datasets of the institution. This helps to understand how data is interconnected and to identify potential impacts in case of modification or deletion of certain datasets.

5. Ensuring quality and consistency of metadata. It is essential to establish guidelines and procedures to ensure the quality and consistency of metadata. This includes defining naming standards, performing periodic validations, and seeking collaboration from all those involved in the creation and maintenance of metadata.

6. Training and qualification of employees. To ensure an effective implementation of metadata management, it is important to invest in training and qualification of the employees involved in this process. They must understand the importance of metadata, how to use it correctly, and how to contribute to its proper maintenance and updating.

2.8.1 Metadata management actors.

Metadata management in the institution's data governance involves several actors who play important roles in the process.

The main ones are:

1. Data Governance Team. The institution's data governance team is responsible for overseeing and coordinating the entire implementation of data governance, including metadata management. This team leads efforts to establish policies, guidelines, and procedures related to metadata management, ensuring the integrity and quality of information.

2. Metadata experts. Metadata specialists are professionals with specific knowledge about creating, using, and managing metadata. They play a crucial role in defining metadata standards, cataloging them, and maintaining the metadata glossary. These experts can also assist in the implementation of metadata management tools and the training of end users.

3. IT professionals. Information technology professionals play a key role in the implementation of metadata management. They are responsible for setting up and maintaining their chosen metadata management tools, ensuring their availability and proper functioning. Additionally, they can assist in integrating existing systems into the metadata management infrastructure.

4. Employees from the business areas. Employees in the institution's business areas are responsible for providing contextual information and knowledge about the data generated and used in their respective areas. They collaborate with the data governance team and metadata experts to identify and document metadata relevant to their processes and activities. These contributors are also responsible for following the policies and guidelines set to ensure the quality and consistency of the metadata.

5. End Users. End users, which include employees of the institution from different areas and departments, use the data and metadata to carry out their daily activities. They are responsible for using metadata management tools to search, consult information about the data, and ensure the correct use of the data in the context of their tasks. They are also responsible for updating metadata as needed.

2.8.2   Key aspects.

Effectively implementing metadata management in institution data governance requires consideration of a few essential prerequisites. Here are the main prerequisites:

1. Definition of relevant metadata. It is crucial to identify and define which metadata is relevant to the institution's data governance. This includes information about the data's origin, context, quality, format, meaning, and other important attributes. This definition involves collaboration between the institution's business areas to ensure a comprehensive and accurate view of the required metadata.

2. Implementation of a metadata management system. To facilitate the management and use of metadata, it is recommended to implement a specific metadata management system.

3. Standardization of terminology and metadata structure. It is important to establish a standardized terminology and a consistent structure for the metadata used. This helps in understanding and interpreting metadata, making it easier to search and share it.

4. Implementation of quality controls and metadata integrity. To ensure the quality and integrity of metadata, it is crucial to establish controls and periodic validation processes. This includes defining formatting rules, performing consistency checks, and setting guidelines for updating and maintaining metadata correctly.

5. Training and qualification of employees. To ensure the effective implementation of metadata management, it is essential to invest in training and qualification of the employees involved. This includes data governance team members, metadata specialists, IT professionals, and end users.

2.9   Implementing data quality management.

Data quality management plays an essential role in the institution's data governance, as it is the guarantee of the reliability and consistency of the information used by the institution. To implement this practice effectively, the institution must follow a few important steps.

Initially, it is necessary to carry out a detailed assessment of the quality of the data available at the institution. This involves identifying errors, inconsistencies, duplications, or gaps in the data. Through this assessment, the institution can better understand data quality issues and prioritize areas that need improvement.

Based on the evaluation carried out, the institution must define clear metrics and criteria for data quality. This includes requirements for data completeness, accuracy, consistency, completeness, and freshness. These metrics and criteria will serve as a benchmark for evaluating and monitoring data quality over time.

Next, it is important to implement processes and quality controls that ensure that the data meets the established criteria. This may involve setting guidelines for collecting, validating, cleaning, and transforming the data, following data quality best practices. The institution may also consider using automated data quality tools to assist in this process.

Another crucial aspect is to define responsibilities and promote collaboration between the areas involved in data management. This includes designating data owners who are responsible for ensuring data quality in their areas. In addition, it is essential to promote awareness of the importance of data quality and encourage collaboration between areas to solve quality problems and share good practices.

Data quality management should be an ongoing process. Therefore, it is important to establish a regular monitoring system to keep track of the quality of the data over time. The institution can invest in monitoring and reporting tools that present key indicators of data quality. Based on this information, the institution will be able to identify areas for improvement and implement corrective actions to constantly raise the quality of the data.

2.9.1   Data quality management actors.

The implementation of data quality management in the institution's data governance requires the participation of different actors, each with its specific role and responsibilities. These actors play a key role in ensuring data quality and the success of governance efforts.

Here are the key players involved in this process:

1. Data Governance Team. The data governance team is responsible for overseeing and coordinating all activities related to data quality management.

This team is made up of experts and leaders who establish policies, guidelines, and strategies for data governance at the institution.

They are responsible for defining data quality objectives, establishing priorities, monitoring results, and supporting and guiding the other areas involved.

2. Data owners. Data owners are the ones responsible for ensuring the quality of the data in their respective areas.

They have in-depth knowledge of the data under their responsibility, including its origin, format, meaning, and context.

Data owners work closely with the data governance team to ensure that the data meets established quality criteria.

3. Data quality experts. Data quality experts have the technical expertise and methodologies to assess, measure, and improve data quality.

They can develop quality strategies, define metrics and criteria, and implement quality processes and controls.

These experts can also provide technical support and training to the other actors involved, ensuring that quality practices are followed correctly.

4. IT professionals. IT professionals play a key role in implementing data quality management.

They are responsible for providing the necessary technological infrastructure, deploying data management systems, and ensuring data integrity and security.

IT professionals can also assist in automating data quality processes and identifying technological solutions to improve data quality and efficiency.

5. End Users. Finally, end users also have an important role in data quality management.

They are the primary beneficiaries of the data and must utilize the quality information to make informed decisions.

End users are responsible for reporting errors or inconsistencies in the data, collaborating on process improvement, and providing feedback to the data governance team.

2.9.2   Key aspects.

Effectively implementing data quality management in institution data governance requires consideration of a few crucial prerequisites.

These prerequisites form the necessary basis to ensure the success of the initiative.

Here are some of the key prerequisites to consider:

1. Commitment from senior management: It is essential that the institution's senior management, including the mayor and key managers, demonstrate full commitment to data quality management.

This high-level involvement is necessary to foster a culture of quality and ensure that the necessary resources are allocated correctly.

Senior management should be actively involved in defining the goals, priorities, and strategies of data governance, recognizing the importance of data quality to the success of municipal initiatives.

2. Proper organizational structure: It is important to establish a clear and appropriate organizational structure for data quality management.

This includes designating a data governance team that is responsible for overseeing and coordinating all activities related to data quality.

The organizational structure must define clear roles and responsibilities for the different actors involved, promoting effective collaboration between the units of the institution.

3. Clear policies and guidelines: The institution should develop clear policies and guidelines for data quality management.

These policies should establish the principles, objectives, and requirements of data quality, providing a solid foundation for all data governance.

The guidelines should guide the processes of collecting, validating, cleaning, and transforming the data, ensuring compliance with data quality best practices.

4. Adequate technological infrastructure: It is important to ensure that the institution has the appropriate systems and tools in place to collect, store, analyze, and monitor data reliably and securely.

The technological infrastructure must meet data quality requirements, ensuring data integrity, consistency, and accessibility.

5. Training and awareness: it is essential to invest in training and awareness of the institution's employees.

Training and workshops should be provided to train employees in relation to data quality best practices.

Additionally, it is necessary to create a culture of quality data, encouraging awareness of the importance of data quality at all levels of the organization.

2.10 Implementing metadata management.

Data governance in the context of artificial intelligence (AI) requires a methodological approach that goes beyond simply organizing and classifying data.

Among the key elements of this process, metadata management stands out, which is an essential activity to ensure the quality, traceability and consistency of the data used in the development and operation of AI-based solutions.

The concept of metadata transcends the technical definition of "data about data" to represent, in practice, the interpretive and descriptive layer that provides meaning and context to the mass of information generated, manipulated, and analyzed within systems.

Metadata management, at its core, consists of the implementation of a coordinated and structured system that allows collecting, storing, organizing, and distributing information about data, its processes, and its uses.

In the AI landscape, this task becomes even more critical, given the volume, variety, and speed at which data is produced and consumed.

The correct implementation of metadata management is a prerequisite for robust data governance, as it not only enables data quality control, but also facilitates transparency, auditability, and compliance with applicable regulations and legislation.

2.10.1 Data Quality Management Actors

Metadata management requires the participation of multiple actors, each with specific responsibilities within the data governance framework. These actors play complementary roles, and the success of management depends on the integration and effective collaboration between them.

Data Governance Team: The data governance team is primarily responsible for establishing the policies, guidelines, and frameworks that guide the collection, storage, and use of metadata.

These professionals must have a strategic vision that covers not only the technical aspects of data management, but also legal and regulatory compliance, which is particularly relevant in a context in which data is increasingly subject to regulations, such as the General Data Protection Regulation (GDPR) in Europe and the General Data Protection Law (LGPD) in Brazil.

The governance team must be able to align metadata strategies with the organization's business objectives, ensuring that AI initiatives operate ethically and effectively.

Data Owners: They are responsible for ensuring the integrity, accuracy, and availability of the data they manage.

Data owners, or "stewards," play a crucial role in metadata governance, as they are the ones who oversee the data lifecycle, ensuring that the information collected, stored, and handled is in accordance with the quality standards set by the organization.

They act as gatekeepers of the data, promoting interoperability and consistency of metadata across different departments and systems.

Data Quality Specialists: Data quality specialists have the technical role of defining standards and metrics for the evaluation and monitoring of metadata quality.

These professionals are essential to ensure that the data used in AI applications is correct, complete, and up-to-date.

The work of these experts is extremely relevant in the context of AI, as the quality of metadata directly affects the performance of machine learning models, which depend on accurate and consistent data to generate reliable results.

IT professionals: The implementation of metadata management requires a robust technological infrastructure, which directly involves information technology professionals.

They are responsible for maintaining and updating metadata management systems, in addition to ensuring that the data platforms used by the organization are secure, scalable, and compatible with the current demands of processing large volumes of data.

Their contribution is indispensable to the smooth functioning of metadata governance in AI, especially in scenarios that require high availability and security.

End Users: Although often underestimated, end users are key players in data governance, as they are the ones who interact directly with information and therefore need accessible and understandable metadata.

They also play an important role in validating the usability of data and metadata, ensuring that the descriptions and contexts provided by the metadata are sufficient for the proper understanding and application of the information.

2.10.2 Key aspects

Effectively implementing metadata management in AI-powered data governance requires considering several key aspects. These factors represent the key prerequisites for the success of a metadata initiative and must be carefully evaluated and planned for by all parties involved.

Commitment from Senior Management: Without the support of senior management, the implementation of metadata management is unlikely to be successful.

Leadership commitment is essential to ensure that policies and practices related to metadata are prioritized within the organization and that the necessary resources are allocated. Management should foster a data culture that values accuracy, transparency, and traceability, and encourages adherence to metadata policies by all levels of the organization.

Appropriate Organizational Structure: Metadata governance requires an organizational structure that is capable of supporting the demands of coordination and communication between the different actors involved in the process.

This includes clearly defining responsibilities and assignments for each team and professional, as well as creating an efficient communication flow between IT, data quality, and end-user departments.

A well-defined framework helps avoid duplication of effort and ensures that metadata initiatives are aligned with the organization's strategic objectives.

Clear Policies and Guidelines: For metadata management to be effective, it is imperative that the organization establishes clear policies and guidelines.

These policies should define how metadata will be collected, stored, categorized, and used, as well as specify the quality standards that must be followed. Clear guidelines also help ensure compliance with laws and regulations, avoiding legal and governance issues.

Adequate Technological Infrastructure: The technological infrastructure is the foundation on which metadata management rests. Appropriate tools and systems are needed to enable the collection and storage of large volumes of metadata efficiently, as well as ensure integration between different data platforms.

Choosing suitable technology solutions, such as metadata management systems (MDMS), is essential to the success of any metadata initiative, especially in the context of AI, where the amount of data processed can be massive.

Training and Awareness: The implementation of effective metadata management also depends on the continuous training of the professionals involved.

All actors, from the governance team to end users, need to be trained to understand the importance of metadata and how to use it appropriately.

Awareness of the value of metadata governance must be disseminated throughout the organization, creating a data culture where the responsible and ethical use of information is a fundamental principle.

3   Conclusion.

Throughout this volume, we explore in a detailed and practical way the key elements for implementing effective data governance in the context of artificial intelligence.

From distinguishing between governance and data management to implementing critical components such as data quality management, information security, metadata, and master data, the book offered a complete roadmap for those who want to structure and organize their data in a way that supports strategic, informed, and secure decisions.

We have learned that data governance is more than a set of good practices — it is the pillar that sustains trust in data and, consequently, the proper functioning of artificial intelligence systems.

Governing data is about ensuring that it is accessible, reliable, and compliant with global and industry regulations, while preserving security and privacy.

Each section of the book was developed with the objective of training professionals to identify the actors and key aspects of each area, leading to efficient, structured and adaptable data management to the demands of the modern market.

However, understanding data governance is only the beginning of a larger, more complex journey. Artificial intelligence, in all its depth and potential, requires an integrated and holistic view to be successful.

This volume is just one step within that essential journey. It is part of the collection "Artificial Intelligence: the Power of Data", which explores, in depth, different aspects of AI and data science.

The two volumes in this collection address equally critical topics, such as the integration of AI systems, predictive analytics, and the use of advanced algorithms for decision-making.

By purchasing and reading the remaining books, you will have the opportunity to develop a thorough and deep understanding that will allow you to not only optimize data governance in your organization, but also harness the full power of artificial intelligence to transform your operations and drive ongoing value.

Invest in your skills, broaden your vision, and get ready to lead digital transformation. The journey is just beginning, and mastery of data and AI is the differentiator that will propel your organization to the next level.

4   Glossary.

"A well-developed glossary is vital to ensure
the clarity and consistency of the terminology
within an organization, facilitating
communication and understanding
among all stakeholders."
Sue Ellen Wright[4]

1   Controlled Access. A security mechanism that restricts access to data or systems to authorized users or processes only. Uses credentials such as passwords, tokens, and certificates.

2   Data Anonymization. Process of removing or changing personal information so that the data subject cannot be directly or indirectly identified.

3   API (Application Programming Interface). A set of programming routines and standards that allows the integration of systems and the sharing of data between different applications.

4   Cloud Storage. Service that allows storing data on remote servers, accessible via the internet, offering scalability and flexibility for storing large volumes of data.

---

[4] Sue Ellen Wright is an expert in terminology and technical translation, a professor at Kent State University, and one of the authors of the "Handbook of Terminology Management." She is important because her work emphasizes the relevance of terminology practices in knowledge management and translation, addressing how the standardization of terms and the creation of glossaries can optimize communication, reduce errors, and increase efficiency in diverse professional and academic contexts.

5   Data Architecture. Organizational structure that defines how data is collected, stored, managed, and used in an organization, aiming to optimize the flow of information.

6   Data Audit. Process of systematic review and evaluation of data and how it is managed, to ensure compliance with governance policies and regulations.

7   National Data Protection Authority (ANPD). Body responsible for the inspection and application of the General Data Protection Law (LGPD) in Brazil, ensuring the protection of personal data.

8   BI (Business Intelligence). Set of technologies and strategies used for business data analysis, providing insights that help in strategic decision-making.

9   Big Data. Extremely large and complex datasets that require advanced technologies for storage, processing, and analysis.

10   Primary Key. A field or group of fields in a database that uniquely identifies each record in a table, ensuring data integrity.

11   Compliance. Compliance with laws, regulations, rules, and internal policies that govern the collection, use, storage, and disposal of data.

12   Data Consistency. Ensuring that data held in different systems or locations is uniform and correct across all its instances.

13   Backup. Data copy made to prevent information loss in the event of a system failure, allowing data recovery.

14   Cryptography. Security technique that encrypts data to protect it against unauthorized access, ensuring confidentiality and integrity.

15 Data Curation. Active data management process to ensure its quality, accessibility, and relevance over time.

16 Data Governance. Set of practices and policies that ensure the responsible and efficient use of data within an organization, covering security, quality, and compliance.

17 Data Lake. Centralized storage of large volumes of unstructured or semi-structured data, used for advanced analytics.

18 Data Steward. Professional responsible for supervising and implementing data governance policies, ensuring their quality and compliance.

19 Data warehouse. Structured data repository that integrates information from multiple sources to support business reporting and analysis.

20 Deduplication. Process of eliminating duplicate records in a database, ensuring the uniqueness and accuracy of the information.

21 Data Development. Activity that involves the creation, maintenance and improvement of data systems, including modeling, integration and updating of databases.

22 Scalability. Ability of a system or process to scale to handle the increased amount of data or users without loss of performance.

23 Foreign Key Structure. A field in a database table that creates a relationship between two tables, connecting them and ensuring the referential integrity of the data.

24 ETL (Extract, Transform, Load). A process that involves extracting data from multiple sources, transforming it into a suitable format, and loading it into a repository such as a data warehouse.

25 GDPR (General Data Protection Regulation). European regulation that defines strict rules for the protection of personal data and the privacy of citizens of the European Union.

26 Data Architecture Management. An activity that involves defining and overseeing an organization's data infrastructure, including the choice of governance technologies, standards, and policies.

27 Content Management. Process of managing documents and unstructured information, such as text files, emails, and images, to ensure their organization and accessibility.

28 Master Data Management (MDM). Practices and processes that ensure that key data (customers, products, suppliers) is consistent, accurate, and up-to-date across the organization.

29 Metadata Management. Data management activity on data, providing information such as the origin, format, structure, and context of data to facilitate its understanding and use.

30 Data Quality Management. Set of practices that ensure the accuracy, integrity, consistency, and relevance of data, minimizing errors and failures in information systems.

31 Data Security Management. Set of practices and technologies used to protect data from unauthorized access, leaks, and other threats to privacy and integrity.

32 Management of Database Management System (DBMS). Administration of the operations of systems that store, manage, and enable efficient access to large volumes of data.

33 Data Governance. Set of practices, processes and organizational structures that ensure the efficient, secure and ethical management of an organization's data.

34 Data Integrity. Quality that ensures that data is correct, consistent, and has not been altered in an unauthorized manner during its transmission or storage.

35 Data Interoperability. Ability of different systems to share, interpret and use data in an integrated and efficient way.

36 LGPD (General Data Protection Law). Brazilian law that regulates the use, collection and processing of personal data, ensuring the privacy and protection of individuals.

37 Metadata. Data that describes other data, providing information such as origin, format, structure, and context, which are essential for the organization and effective use of data.

38 Data Modeling. The process of creating abstract representations that define the structure and relationships between different data elements in a system.

39 Continuous Data Monitoring. Process of continuous verification of data quality, integrity and security to identify and correct problems in real time.

40 Normalization. The process of organizing data in a database, eliminating redundancies and ensuring that data is stored efficiently and consistently.

41 NoSQL. A category of database that does not use the traditional relational model, allowing the storage and manipulation of large volumes of unstructured data.

42 Pseudonymization. A technique that replaces identifiable data with a pseudonym, ensuring the protection of privacy, but allowing the use of data for analysis.

43 Data Quality. A set of attributes that determine the reliability of data, such as accuracy, completeness, timeliness, and relevance.

44 Data Model Ranking. Evaluation of different data models in terms of their efficiency, ability to scale, and meet organizational requirements.

45 Functional Requirements. Specifications that define the functions and behaviors that a system or application must perform, usually related to data processing.

46 Non-functional requirements. Criteria that define how a system should operate, including aspects such as performance, security, scalability, and reliability.

47 Information Security. Set of practices and technologies that protect data and information against unauthorized access, misuse, interruptions and damage.

48 SLA (Service Level Agreement). Formal agreement between service provider and customer, which defines the expected service levels, including availability and performance of data systems.

49 SQL (Structured Query Language). A programming language used to manage and query data in relational database systems.

50 Data Steward. Professional responsible for ensuring that data is managed ethically, efficiently, and in compliance with the organization's policies.

51 Quality Check Table. Tool used to audit data quality, evaluating various criteria such as consistency, completeness, and compliance with governance policies.

52 Digital Transformation. The process of integrating digital technologies into all areas of an organization, fundamentally changing the way the company operates and delivers value.

53 Data Validation. Verification process to ensure that data is correct, accurate, and in compliance with business rules and system requirements.

54 Web Service. A service based on web standards, which allows interoperability between systems, facilitating the exchange of data and communication between applications on different platforms.

5   References.

ABITEBOUL, S.; HULL, R.; VIANU, V. (1995). Foundations of Databases. Addison-Wesley.

B. SETTLES, Active learning literature survey, Technical Report, University of Wisconsin-Madison D partment of Computer Sciences, 2009.

BERTINO, E.; SANDHU, R. (2005). Database Security – Concepts, Approaches, and Challenges. IEEE Computer Society.

CHEN, M.; MAO, S.; LIU, Y. (2014). Big Data: A Survey. Springer.

Data Management Association International (DAMA). (2020). "Data Governance Best Practices for NoSQL Databases and Graphs". DAMA White Paper Series, 7.

DAVENPORT, T.H., & DYCHE, J. (2013). Big Data in Big Companies. Harvard Business Review, 91(6), 60-68.

DOU, W.; XU, L.; ZHANG, Z. (2017). Big Data and Smart Service Systems. Springer.

ECK, D. M. (2019). Governance of Data: Implementing Data Governance Programs. Wiley.

EMERSON, D. (2015). The Data Governance Imperative: A Guide to Aligning Data Governance with Business Strategy. Wiley.

FERNÁNDEZ-MACÍAS, E.; GRAHAM, M.; LUCIANO, F. (2020). The Ethics of Artificial Intelligence in the Age of Digital Capitalism. Oxford University Press.

FLORES, A. W.; BEYNON-DAVIES, P. (2020). Data Governance: How to Design, Deploy, and Sustain an Effective Data Governance Program. Springer.

FRANK, M.; RONEN, B.; VARDI, G. (2018). Data Governance: A Practitioner's Guide to Data Management and Governance. Wiley.

GARTNER, L.; KAMINSKY, M. (2018). Implementing Effective Data Governance: A Guide to Unlocking Value from Data Assets. McGraw-Hill.

GOERTZEL, B. (2014). Artificial general intelligence: concept, state of the art, and future prospects. Journal of Artificial General Intelligence, 5(1), 1.

HALL, P.; ALUR, R.; HAWKING, S. (2015). Artificial Intelligence: Foundations of Computational Agents. Cambridge University Press.

HARDING, L. (2017). The Data Governance Framework: How to Design, Build, and Sustain an Effective Data Governance Program. Wiley.

HASHEM, I. A. T.; YAZDI, M.; CHEN, C. (2018). The Role of Big Data and AI in Transforming Business Governance: Impacts and Ethical Challenges. Wiley.

HEINEMANN, K.; ALLERT, J. (2020). Big Data Governance: The Role of Governance in Big Data and Artificial Intelligence Projects. Springer.

HUANG, G.; SHAH, S. (2019). Artificial Intelligence for Data-Driven Decisions: Best Practices and Case Studies. Oxford University Press.

IMHOFF, C. (2020). Holistic Approach to Data Governance for AI. Boulder BI Brain Trust.

JOHNSON, M. (2018). Data Quality: A Key Factor in Machine.

JONES, A. et al. (2018). "Implementing Data Governance in a NoSQL Graph Database Environment". Proceedings of the International Conference on Data Management, 132-145.

KAPLAN, A.; HAENLEIN, M. (2019). Artificial Intelligence: A Guide for Thinking Humans. Oxford University Press.

KITCHIN, R. (2014). The Data Revolution: Big Data, Open Data, Data Infrastructures and Their Consequences. SAGE Publications.

LADLEY, J. (2019). Data Governance: How to Design, Deploy, and Sustain an Effective Data Governance Program. Oxford, UK: Elsevier.

MAYER-SCHÖNBERGER, V.; CUKIER, K. (2013). Big Data: A Revolution That Will Transform How We Live, Work, and Think. Houghton Mifflin Harcourt.

MILLER, S. M. (2018). The Practical Guide to Data Governance: How to Design, Implement, and Sustain an Effective Data Governance Program. Addison-Wesley.

REDMAN, R T.C. (2008). Data Governance. Bridgewater, NJ: Technics Publications.

REDMAN, T.C. & SOARES, D. D. (2021). Application of AI in Data Governance. AI Magazine, 37(4), 78-85.

SOARES, S. (2013). Big Data Governance: An Emerging Imperative. MC Press.

WESKE, M. (2019). Business Process Management: Concepts, Languages, Architectures. Springer.

WIECZOREK, M., & MERTENS, P. (2019). Data Governance: A Practical Guide. Englewood Cliffs, NJ: Prentice Hall.

ZHU, H.; GRANT, D. (2019). Building a Data Governance Framework: A Practitioner's Guide for Managing Data as a Strategic Asset. Wiley.

"Every great dream begins with a dreamer. Always remember that you have within you the strength, patience, and passion to reach for the stars to change the world."

Harriet Tubman[5]

---

[5] Harriet Tubman (née Araminta Ross; c. 1820 or 1821 – March 10, 1913) was an American abolitionist and political activist. Born into slavery, Tubman escaped and subsequently went on about thirteen missions to rescue approximately seventy enslaved people, including family and friends, using the network of anti-slavery activists and safe houses known as the Underground Railroad. During the American Civil War, she served as a spy for the Union army. After the war, Tubman was an activist in the women's suffrage movement.

6   Artificial Intelligence Collection: the power of data.

The collection, written by Prof. Marcão, offers a deep immersion in the universe of Artificial Intelligence (AI), a technology that is transforming the world irreversibly. In a series of carefully crafted books, the author explores complex concepts in an accessible way, providing the reader with a broad understanding of AI and its impact on modern societies.

The central goal of the collection is to empower the reader to understand what is behind the technology that drives today's world, from its practical applications in everyday life to the ethical and philosophical debates that emerge as AI advances.

Each volume focuses on specific and fundamental aspects of the theme, with explanations based on both academic research and the author's practical experience, making the work indispensable for anyone who wants to navigate this field essential to the future.

6.1   Why study the ARTIFICIAL INTELLIGENCE AND THE POWER OF DATA collection?

We are experiencing an unprecedented technological revolution, where AI plays a central role in sectors such as medicine, entertainment, finance, education, and government.

With a writing that combines clarity and depth, Prof. Marcão's collection makes the topic accessible to both laymen and specialists.

In addition to exploring facts, the work offers reflections on the social, cultural, and ethical impact of AI, encouraging the reader to rethink their relationship with technology.

6.2   Who is the collection suitable for?

The collection "ARTIFICIAL INTELLIGENCE AND THE POWER OF DATA" is aimed at a wide range of readers. Tech professionals will find deep technical insights, while students and the curious will have access to clear and accessible explanations.

Managers, business leaders, and policymakers will also benefit from AI's strategic understanding, which is essential for making informed decisions.

Prof. Marcão offers a complete approach, addressing both technical aspects and the strategic implications of AI in the current scenario.

6.3   The intellectual and practical value of the collection.

More than a series of technical books, this collection is a tool for intellectual transformation. Prof. Marcão invites the reader to reflect on the future of humanity in a world where machines and algorithms are increasingly present in our lives.

7 The books of the Collection.

7.1 Data, information and knowledge.

This book essentially explores the theoretical and practical foundations of Artificial Intelligence, from data collection to its transformation into intelligence.

Focusing on machine learning, AI training, and neural networks, the work is indispensable for professionals and scholars seeking to understand the challenges and opportunities of AI.

7.2 Data into gold: how to turn information into wisdom in the age of AI.

This book looks at the evolution of artificial intelligence from raw data to building artificial wisdom, combining neural networks, deep learning, and knowledge modeling.

With practical examples in healthcare, finance, and education, and addressing ethical and technical challenges, it is ideal for anyone seeking to understand the transformative impact of AI.

7.3 Challenges and limitations of data in AI.

The book offers an in-depth analysis of the role of data in the development of AI exploring topics such as quality, bias, privacy, security, and scalability.

With practical case studies in healthcare, finance, and public safety, it is an essential guide for professionals and researchers seeking to understand how data shapes the future of artificial intelligence.

7.4   Historics are not a thing of the past.

This book explores how data management, especially historical data, is critical to the success of AI projects. It addresses the relevance of ISO standards to ensure quality and safety, in addition to analyzing trends and innovations in data processing.

With a practical approach, it is an indispensable resource for professionals focused on efficient data management in the age of AI.

7.5   Controlled vocabulary.

This comprehensive guide looks at the advantages and challenges of implementing controlled vocabularies in the context of AI and information science.

With a detailed approach, it covers everything from the naming of data elements to the interactions between semantics and cognition. Essential for professionals and researchers looking to optimize data management and the development of AI systems.

7.6   Data Management for AI.

The book presents advanced strategies for transforming raw data into powerful insights, with a focus on meticulous curation and efficient management.

In addition to technical solutions, it addresses ethical and legal issues, empowering the reader to face the complex challenges of information.

Whether you're a manager, data scientist, or AI enthusiast, and for professionals looking to master data management in the digital age.

7.7   Information architecture.

Essential guide for professionals who want to master data management in the digital age, combining theory and practice to create efficient and scalable AI systems.

With insights into modeling, ethical and legal challenges, it is ideal for data scientists, AI engineers, and IT managers looking to turn data into actionable intelligence and gain competitive advantage.

7.8   Fundamentals.

Essential work for those who want to master the key concepts of AI, with an accessible approach and practical examples.

The book explores innovations such as Machine Learning and Natural Language Processing, as well as ethical and legal challenges, and offers a clear view of the impact of AI on various industries, ideal for professionals and technology enthusiasts.

7.9   Large language models – LLMs.

Essential guide to understanding the language model revolution (LLMs) in AI.

The book explores the evolution of GPTs and the latest innovations in human-computer interaction, offering practical insights into their impact on industries such as healthcare, education, and finance. Indispensable for professionals, researchers, and AI enthusiasts.

7.10 Machine learning.

This book is essential for professionals and enthusiasts who want to master revolutionary areas of AI. It offers a comprehensive overview of supervised and unsupervised algorithms, deep neural networks, and federated learning.

With discussions on the ethics and explainability of models, it prepares the reader for the challenges and opportunities of AI in sectors such as healthcare, finance, and public safety.

7.11 Synthetic minds.

A must-read for anyone looking to explore the future of generative AIs, this book reveals how these "synthetic minds" are redefining creativity, work, and human interactions.

Aimed at technology professionals, content creators, and the curious, it offers an in-depth analysis of the challenges and opportunities of these technologies, reflecting on their impact on society.

7.12 The issue of copyright.

This book is a thought-provoking invitation to explore the future of creativity in a world where humans and machines collaborate, addressing questions about authorship, originality, and intellectual property in the age of generative AIs.

Ideal for professionals, creators and innovation enthusiasts, it offers deep reflections and challenges you to rethink the balance between technology and creators' rights.

7.13 Questions and Answers from Basics to Complex – Volumes 1 to 4.

The questions, organized into 4 volumes, are essential practical guides to master the main concepts of AI. The 1121 questions address topics such as Machine Learning, Natural Language Processing and Computer Vision, offering clear and concise answers.

Ideal for professionals, students, and enthusiasts, the book combines didactic explanations with insights into ethics, data privacy, and the challenges of AI helping to transform your knowledge and explore the potential of this revolutionary technology.

Part 1 includes:

- Information, data and geoprocessing.
- Evolution of artificial intelligence.
- AI milestones.
- Basic concepts and definitions.

Part 2 includes:

- Complex concepts.
- Machine learning.
- Natural language processing.
- Computer vision and robotics.
- Decision algorithms.

Part 3 includes:

- Data privacy.
- Automation of work.
- Large-scale language models - LLMs.

Part 4 includes:

- The role of data in the age of artificial intelligence.

- Fundamentals of artificial intelligence.
- Government, politics and the fight against corruption.
- Mental health.

7.14   Glossary.

With more than a thousand concepts selected from the context of artificial intelligence clearly explained, the book addresses topics such as Machine Learning, Natural Language Processing, Computer Vision and AI Ethics.

Ideal for professionals and the curious, the work offers a comprehensive overview of the impact of AI on society.

- Part 1 contemplates concepts starting with the letters A to D.
- Part 2 contemplates concepts initiated by the letters E to M.
- Part 3 contemplates concepts starting with the letters N to Z.

7.15   Prompt engineering: volumes 1 to 6.

The collection covers all the fundamental themes of prompt engineering, providing a complete professional development.

With a rich variety of prompts for areas such as leadership, digital marketing, and information technology, it offers practical examples to improve clarity, decision-making, and gain valuable insights.

Ideal for professionals, entrepreneurs, and students, this guide reveals how to use the power of prompts to turn ideas into concrete actions and drive impressive results.

The volumes cover the following subjects:

- Volume 1: deals with the fundamentals. structuring concepts and history of prompt engineering.
- Volume 2: Covers Tools and Technologies, State and Context Management, and Ethics and Security.

- Volume 3: Looks at language models, tokenization, and training methods.
- Volume 4: will teach you the techniques to ask correct questions.
- Volume 5: presents and analyzes case studies and errors.
- Volume 6: is your essential guide with the best prompts.

With an extensive collection of practical prompts, the book offers everything from tips for effective communication and decision-making to suggestions for personal development, career, marketing, and information technology.

7.16   Guide to Being a Prompt Engineer – Volumes 1 and 2.

The collection explores the advanced fundamentals and skills required to be a successful prompt engineer, highlighting the benefits, risks, and the critical role this role plays in the development of artificial intelligence.

Volume 1 covers crafting effective prompts, and volume 2 is your guide to understanding and applying the fundamentals of Prompt Engineering.

For those looking to optimize their interactions with AI, the book is a must-have for technology professionals.

7.17   Data governance.

Find out how to implement effective data governance with this comprehensive collection. Offering practical guidance, the books range from data architecture management to protection and quality, providing a complete view for transforming data into strategic assets.

Volume 1 addresses practices and regulations. Volume 2 explores in depth the processes, techniques, and best practices for conducting effective audits on data models. Volume 3 is your definitive guide to deploying data governance with AI.

Ideal for IT specialists, managers, and enthusiasts, it is the definitive resource to ensure compliance, security, and efficiency in data management.

7.18   Algorithm Governance.

This book analyzes the impact of algorithms on society, exploring everything from their foundations to ethical and regulatory issues.

It addresses transparency, accountability, and bias, with practical solutions for auditing and monitoring algorithms in sectors such as finance, health, and education.

Ideal for professionals and managers, it offers an ethical and sustainable view of digital governance.

7.19   From IT to AI: the transition guide.

For Information Technology professionals, the transition to AI represents an opportunity to enhance their skills and contribute to the development of innovative solutions that drive the future.

In this book, we explore the reasons for making this transition, the essential skills, a practical roadmap, and the prospects for the future of the IT job market.

Ideal for IT professionals who want to make a career transition to being an artificial intelligence professional.

7.20   Intelligent leadership with AI - transform your team and drive results

This book reveals how artificial intelligence can revolutionize team management and maximize organizational performance.

By combining traditional leadership techniques with AI-powered insights, you'll learn how to optimize processes, make more strategic decisions, and create more efficient and engaged teams.

Aimed at managers, business leaders, consultants, and professionals who want to improve their leadership skills in an increasingly digital world, this book offers practical and accessible strategies for implementing AI in the day-to-day of team management. If you're looking to take your team to the next level, this is the essential guide.

7.21 Impacts and transformations.

The collection covers everything from the technical and ethical challenges of detecting AI-generated text, to the influence of algorithms on our digital lives and the transformation of content creation.

The collection also discusses the future of humanity in light of the technological singularity and the dangers of disinformation in the digital age, where artificial intelligence can be used to manipulate public opinion.

1. Volume 1: Challenges and Solutions in the Detection of AI-generated texts.
2. Volume 2: The Age of Filter Bubbles.
3. Volume 3: Content Creation.
4. Volume 4: The singularity is near.
5. Volume 5: Real Stupidity Versus Artificial Intelligence
6. Volume 6: The Age of Stupidity: A Cult of Stupidity.
7. Volume 7: Autonomy on the move: the smart vehicle revolution.
8. Volume 8: Poiesis and creativity with AI.

Ideal for IT professionals, politicians, academics, urban planners and technology enthusiasts, the collection reveals the social, economic and ethical impacts of this transformation, addressing the reconfiguration of society, cities and the labor market.

"In the information age, knowledge is power, but true wisdom lies in the ability to discern and wisely utilize the vastness of available data."

Brian Herbert[6]

[6] American author known for his works in the field of science fiction, especially for having co-written several works set in the universe created by his father, Frank Herbert, in the "Dune" book series.

8 Meet the author. A researcher always in search of knowledge.

I'm Marcus Pinto, known as Prof. Marcão, a specialist in information technology, information architecture and artificial intelligence. With a solid career, I bring you this collection of books, the result of extensive research and study, with the aim of making technical knowledge accessible and applicable.

My experience as a consultant, educator and writer and as an information architecture analyst for more than 40 years allows me to work in strategic areas, offering innovative solutions that meet the growing needs of the technological market.

Over decades, I have developed expertise in data, information, and artificial intelligence, crucial areas for the creation of robust systems that process the immensity of data generated in the contemporary world.

With works available on Amazon, I offer content that addresses topics such as Data Governance, Big Data and Artificial Intelligence, always focused on practical application and strategic vision.

Author of more than 150 books, he studies the impact of artificial intelligence in various fields, from its technical foundations to the ethical implications of its use.

In my lectures and mentorships, I share not only the relevance of AI, but also the challenges and precautions necessary for an ethical and responsible adoption of these technologies.

Technological evolution is inevitable, and my books offer the way for those who wish to not only understand, but master the future. With a focus on education and human development, I invite you to explore this transformative journey through my works.

9 How to contact prof. Marcão.

9.1 For lectures, training and business mentoring.

marcao.tecno@gmail.com

Consulting and Training Company: https://mvpconsult.com.br

9.2 Prof. Marcão on Linkedin.

https://bit.ly/linkedin_profmarcao